How President Trump Will Win the War on Christmas

Sec. Derrick S. Johnson

Introduction

Christmas is back! The Commander-in-Chief is on our side, and on Christmas' side, for the first time since the attacks from liberals began decades ago. Why will President Trump be the first president who will be able to win the war on Christmas? It simple—he's the first president, and one of the precious few leaders in all of Washington, to acknowledge that there is a war on the most sacred and cherished holiday in this country's history. He knows that this war us real, and he promises, "We're saying merry Christmas again" now that he's president.

President Trump knows why the heart of America has been broken for decades. Traditions have been undergoing scrutiny under the microscope of political correctness for many years, and some of them are barely hanging on. Cultural revivals are honored over the world, with one exception: conservative America. *Liberals are so quick to honor any cultural traditions that are fading from the world scene*, but since many of them were raised in Christian households, they are far too eager to flush anything that represents conservative Christian values down the drain. We can only assume that most liberals did not get their favorite gift one Christmas, back in 1989, and they have had a secret resentment toward the holiday ever since.

Well, you are about to see the return of America's most cherished family traditions. It will be spun on liberal media as a racist, xenophobic step in the wrong direction, but don't believe it. It is a revival of cultural values that the President has ushered in, and it is time that Americans, while respecting other holidays of course, reclaim their right to live their holiday out loud. As the President recently told a crowd of supporters in Wisconsin, "You go to the department stores and they'll say, 'Happy New Year,' or they'll say other things and it'll be in red—they'll have it painted— but they don't say... Well, guess what? We're saying 'Merry Christmas' again!"

The History of Christmas in America

The War on Christmas is not a new war, but the enemy is new. Gone are the days of peacefully celebrating the birth of Jesus, sprinkled with a little Santa Claus, and family gatherings around the tree. Or are those days completely gone? No, thankfully, there are plenty of people still around who can testify to the fact that Christmas, more than any other holiday, is more than just a religious institution, it is the cornerstone holiday of American culture. In the early days of America, only certain sects, like those of strict Puritan heritage, expressed disdain for Christmas. Now, there is a group rising in the country that not only wants to remove Jesus from Christmas, but would be more than happy to see it replaced with a generic winter celebration representing all faiths. This new group of P.C. police have also perfected the art of self-righteousness, if for no other reason than to run from their own Christian roots in search of a more "accepting" way to celebrate. The sad truth is that they are ignoring the most accepting message in all of

American history: Christmas is about the birth of Jesus, the newborn savior of mankind, who died for all people, not just Americans in the Bible Belt, but all people. He was born to an unwed mother, which the world sees as shameful, but all of this sets the stage for the most awe-inspiring component of Christmas: the face of God in an infant savior.

The enemy is not Hannukah, or Kwanzaa, or Ramadan. Those attacking Christmas are not the Muslims, Jews, or Jehovah's Witnesses. The enemy has been right in front of us all the time: the liberal media. Every Christmas you see the same story play out:

The holidays are demonized for becoming too commercialized, Americans are made to feel guilty for excessive eating or drinking, and now back to our Holiday Special, *The Lorax*. Oh great, now we can feel guilty about using a real Christmas tree this year.

While this may have started as an honest attempt to appeal to America's ever-growing diversity, it has taken on a life of its own. After years of these Christmas-demonizing news stories and documentaries, we are being made to feel ashamed of a holiday simply because it does not make any appeal to the Jewish and Muslim population, or because it has religious roots and is thick with religious symbolism. There is no other country in the world who loves to hate its own traditions more than liberal America, and Christmas is, every single year, the easiest target.

During the era of the American Civil War, many Northerners thought celebrating Christmas was sinful. Alabama, Louisiana, and Arkansas were the first to make Christmas a legal holiday. The overly-religious folks that waged war on America's most-loved holiday were the first to lose the battle on American soil. The North may have won the war against a divided nation, but the ultra-strict Puritan prudes of the North lost the battle against Christmas.

During the years of Reconstruction, 1860-1870, America was not only reconstructing the nation's roads and bridges, it was also piecing together a common fabric from which the future could be built. Holidays were always treated with reverence and respect, especially when it came to Christmas, and no better day could represent the healing and forgiveness our country needed than Christmas. A time of giving, sharing, being around those you love, and reuniting with family.

This is when Christmas truly became a national holiday. From Virginia to the Territory of Arizona, New Hampshire to Alabama, this was the day that we chose as a developing country to represent our core values of love and selfless giving.

The modern skeptical view of Christmas disregards this part of its history. We never hear these stories in school. We hear how religious minorities celebrate their unique holidays, and how winter holidays are celebrated over the world, but we don't talk much about how meaningful Christmas is in the history of America. Why are we so quick to throw it out? It is so full of meaning, so rich in American culture, and so flawlessly anchored in the highest of human values, love. You do not need to be a Christian in order to appreciate the holiday either, enough of it is secular in nature. Rudolph, Santa, Elves, Mrs. Claus, making or buying gifts for each other, Christmas trees, gingerbread houses, Frosty the Snowman, and at least two weeks off of school. There's enough for even an atheist to enjoy. Even more for the Christian.

No other holiday uniquely captures the capitalist sentiment better than Christmas either. It gets most people off of their couch and into local businesses, whether to stuff a stocking, prove to your loved one that you've been listening to them all year, or even to give an extra donation to a charity that is helping the less fortunate. Christmas even keeps the economy going, giving even the most Jewish or Muslim of business owners a reason to smile.

It is always trendy for spoiled Americans to show contempt for their own family traditions, and Christmas was an exception until the 1970s and 1980s, when even the most beloved of holidays became the target of ridicule and trendy, cultural self-hate. While I believe that eventually people overcome their bitterness, some unresolved resentment toward the most magical of holidays may keep people away for most of their adult lives. Maybe Christmas represents the closed-minded family they ran away from, or the hand-me-downs they were too embarrassed to wear to church, but as people grow up they begin to realize that all of this hub-bub was real, and it wasn't really about Santa Claus the whole time. In fact, for many of us, Christmas had very little to do with the God of our church. The real meaning has been in the end, not the means. The end has been an annual excuse to gather as a family, set our differences aside, and remind the people we love that it's not too much effort to show it.

"How times have changed-- but you know what? Now they are changing back again, just remember that."

-President Donald Trump

<u>What is The War on Christmas?</u>

Did you know that by the 1920s, the face of St. Nick was almost always portrayed as the fat jolly name in a red and white suit in movies, television, and advertisements. How ironic that this same media would one day be complaining about the commercialization of Christmas. The war against Christmas is, of course, not actually a war. It is also not anti-American to protest at Christmas, but we would be literally protesting against ourselves. Where can the spirit of Christmas come from if not from our own heart? Some people live through many Christmases where this was all they had to hold on to. My uncle used to say he was so poor when he was a kid, he had to poop in the bathtub in order to have anything to play with. I never understood that, but then I learned my uncle used to be a woman.

Isaiah 9:6 - For unto us a child is born, unto us a son is given: and the government shall be upon his shoulder: and his name shall be called Wonderful, Counsellor, The mighty God, The everlasting Father, The Prince of Peace.

<u>John 3:16</u> - For God so loved the world, that he gave his only begotten Son, that whosoever believeth in him should not perish, but have everlasting life.

<u>Matthew 1:18-25</u> - Now the birth of Jesus Christ was on this wise: When as his mother Mary was espoused to Joseph, before they came together, she was found with child of the Holy Ghost.
 (Read More...)

<u>Acts 20:35</u> - I have shewed you all things, how that so labouring ye

ought to support the weak, and to remember the words of the Lord Jesus, how he said, It is more blessed to give than to receive.

John 1:14 - And the Word was made flesh, and dwelt among us, (and we beheld his glory, the glory as of the only begotten of the Father,) full of grace and truth.

Matthew 2:11 - And when they were come into the house, they saw the young child with Mary his mother, and fell down, and worshipped him: and when they had opened their treasures, they presented unto him gifts; gold, and frankincense, and myrrh.

<u>Jeremiah 29:11</u> - For I know the thoughts that I think toward you, says the LORD, thoughts of peace, and not of evil, to give you an expected end.

<u>Luke 6:38</u> - Give, and it shall be given unto you; good measure, pressed down, and shaken together, and running over, shall men give into your bosom. For with the same measure that ye mete withal it shall be measured to you again.

(all Bible quotes are from the *Authorized King James Version*)

What could possibly be worth fighting about? Even in the most religious context, this beautiful holiday is the least offensive tradition in America. In fact, ask anyone (except atheists), whether or not they are offended by someone saying, "Merry Christmas." They aren't. They would expect any country to hold on to traditions with all their might, and they find it funny that Americans change it to "Happy Holidays," as if they are going to great lengths to be so culturally sensitive. Many visiting foreigners have told me that Christmas in America is one of the most beautiful holidays they know of, often adding a reference to an old Christmas movie favorite. It has romance, laughter, family craziness, and childhood magic.

Why would we sit back and allow this amazing holiday to be pulled out from under us while we sit, distracted, in front of the liberal media, listening to their politically correct insanity being poured over the masses like a wave of nonsensical rhythms beating into our heads in a constant rhythm of hopelessness and fear?

Bill O'Reilly was not just creating

an intriguing story when he reported on the assaults on Christmas nation-wide, he has as much interest in saving a Christian holiday as your Aunt Ruth has in putting her change in the Salvation Army's holiday spittoon. He was really just being the grumpy old man on television complaining about how much things around him have changed. I recall how even my saint of a grandmother was a little irritated that the tree-lined streets of rural Stockton had been turned into a giant concrete collection of on-ramps and off-ramps.

The war is real. It is now. It is on every street corner and on every social media app. We must not let the liberal media win this one. If you follow my plan below, you will not only have a deeper sense of Christmas in your own life, but you will see why it is worth saving!

TIP: If a family member argues about the religious history of Christmas and/or tries to make this a religious discussion, but you know they have been chanting Buddhism or something lately, then just tell them it's Jesus birthday and he doesn't like to talk about religion. Then, tell that family member how great the egg nog is, and ask if they've tried it yet. If they still don't get the hint, just act interested, do not engage, and at first opportunity slip into the kitchen and re-live some strange fuzzy memory with Aunt Linda.

3. Why Liberals Hate Christmas

Luke 10:38 - 10:42

"Now it came to pass, as they went, that he entered into a certain village: and a certain woman named Martha received him into her house. And she had a sister called Mary, which also sat at Jesus' feet, and heard his word. But Martha was cumbered about

much serving, and came to him, and said, Lord, dost thou not care that my sister hath left me to serve alone? Bid her, therefore, that she help me. And Jesus answered and said unto her, Martha, Martha, thou art careful and troubled about many things: But one thing is needful: and Mary hath chosen that good part, which shall not be taken away from her."

Make no mistake, many liberals despise Christmas with all of their might. Not Jewish liberals. Not Muslim liberals. Not gay liberals. The liberals who hate Christmas are the liberals who had a bad experience with Christmas in their childhood. Maybe they messed up during a church play, and it has been haunting them ever since. Maybe a relative died near the holidays, and it was the only relative that wasn't physically abusive. Maybe that was the day their dad stabbed them in the leg with a corn-cob holder and never said he was sorry. Whatever the reason, they want to fake some sort of religious sensitivity outrage in order to ruin everyone's holiday.

Are those who have made it their mission to destroy Christmas going to stop? There's really only one way to stop it, and it will freeze everyone in their tracks. The enemy will be destroyed forever, and Christmas will be restored to its loftiest position on the calendar.

<u>TIP</u>: Make a new family rule that whoever complains about the environmental impact of this year's Christmas tree has to buy the tree next year. Along with the tree, and this is the most important, they must provide every family member with a detailed brochure explaining why the tree they brought is the best environmental choice. The brochure must include an anonymous survey of every family member as to whether Christmas was more (or less) magical as a result of an eco-friendly tree.

Sec. Derrick S. Johnson

Liberals never hate Christmas for the reasons they say. They'll concoct some story out of a string of historical facts. They hate Christmas because Christmas probably sucked when they were a kid. Just keep that in mind while we fight this war.

President Trump and the Art of *Christmas* Warfare

10 Steps to Christmas Victory

President Trump's *Art of the Deal* gives us a clear idea as to how he plans to fight the War on Christmas. Using the basic concepts outlined in his book, I will imagine a list of methods he will use to win this war.

1.<u>We should think big.</u> We will not win a war on Christmas by underestimating the threat, and a small solution would be tragic.

The solution needs to be big—
yuge—if we want to win this!

2.<u>Prepare for the worst.</u> If you are
prepared to have to fight this war
under the guise of a culture
warrior, then you are ready to
hear my plan, because yours is
the worst.

3.<u>If you own a casino, don't
gamble</u>. Don't start investing in
Christmas decorations, they never
appreciate if they are bought
from a store. They always have
appreciative value if they are
handmade.

4.<u>Be flexible</u>. You need to be able
to approach this from any angle.
Learn a little something about

Hannukah or Ramadan or some other culture's December holiday. It may have nothing to do with Christmas, but knowing a little something never hurts.

5.<u>Use your leverage</u>. If you have a seat on the city council, you could throw that in your cousin's face at Christmas.

6.<u>Know your market</u>. Who is the enemy to Christmas, remember? The liberal media. The sad thing is that we can't make them not-liberal, so we will have to send our front line to the battle that could use us most, our family. Cousin Patsy hates Christmas? Kill her with kindness and get her an extra-fancy Christmas card, and include the biggest bill you can afford. (I would think less than $100 might be considered an insult)

7.<u>Enhance your location</u>. For me, this would mean parking away from all the cars so as not to get pinned-in during any kind of Christmas party, but also in order to make a better entrance. For an approach that is non-specific to a location, try Christmas cards or a text. Remind your family of the importance of this war.

8.<u>Get the word out</u>. This war is not one of countries, but of propaganda. Recruit family members to join the cause. Have you considered making a

Facebook page for your family Christmas party? How about your work Christmas party? Ask your boss if you can be in charge of setting up a Facebook page for your work party, then instead of calling it the company "holiday" party, rename it. I'm sure you'll think of something Christmasey, think big! (Ex: "Bullhead City Plumbing's Santa-Meets-Jesus Christmas Celebration")

9.<u>Prepare to get excited.</u> Use hyperbole to get a reaction from the masses. This is less relevant to the topic of holidays and more of a moment where you just realize that President Trump has been joking this entire time.

10.<u>Be prepared to fight back</u>. Not physically, of course, but with witty retorts and fake outrage. "This is a real war!" or, "Why are you always insisting that I should have just stayed home on voting day? It hurts my feelings!"

These are the scenarios that I believe we will finally be empowered to help the president with based on his book. I realize now that this is not what I said I would be listing, but it takes a lot of effort to go all the way back up the page to delete what I've written there. It would take time, and time is something we DON'T have. We must prepare to fight, December will be here in four days (or whatever day it is where you are, bless your soul). Don't give up for a moment, or you may never smell another pine cone.

<u>Doing Your Part as a Defender of Christmas</u>

There is always something you can do to help your country in time of need. The second president of the United States, John Adams, was an ardent supporter of the country he helped to found. We see this so clearly in his Novangelus Essay Number 1, written in 1774. James Madison also stated, "**Unless some amicable & adequate arrangements be speedily taken for adjusting all the subsisting accounts and discharging the**

public engagements, a dissolution of the union will be inevitable...”

On the lines below, list all the ways you can help prevent our union from dissolving:

1.___________________________

2.___________________________

3.___________________________

4.___________________________

5.___________________________

6.___________________________

7.___________________________

8.___________________________

9.___________________________

10._________________________________

11._________________________________

12._________________________________

13._________________________________

14._________________________________

15._________________________________

16._________________________________

17._________________________________

Why Every Country Defends Its Traditions

Traditions have been around a long time, and for good reason. They work! Often there is a reason for it, such as the healing power of pumpkins at Halloween, but usually they are symbols that we use to connect us to the previous generation. Without tradition, there would be very little symbology left in the world. We can see it fading with each generation.

Egyptians used to build pyramids once a year. They wouldn't change this tradition just because a bunch of young Egyptians started complaining about how it, well, you know the rest. Without hesitation, those were torn down at once. Every pyramid, wiped from the face of the earth, never to be seen again. We can only imagine how grand they were, some over seven meters high, and each one demonstrating the Egyptian people's mastery over a specific three-dimensional shape. This is what happens when a country doesn't hold on dearly to every tradition.

The Best Defense is a Good Offense

A culture war cannot be won by any group of people not willing to fight for it. Are we worshiping the birth of a helpless infant, or God in-the-flesh, able-to-rip-his-enemy-to-shreds-if-he-wants-to Christ Baby? Excuse my language, but it's time for Christmas to grow some bells. Without everyone's participation, this war will be won by the dark side of humanity. We cannot let this happen.

You may be wondering, what kind of *offense* am I suggesting? Nothing less than the full-blown, hard-and-fast approach. I have developed a simple 2-step plan for getting Christmas back.

<u>Step 1:</u> The moment you discover someone doesn't like Christmas, shower them with gifts, and win them back to Christmas' side. This doesn't work on most people of another religion, because they never hated Christmas. Remember, the only people who really hate Christmas are those who's childhood Christmases sucked. Find them, and reverse the process.

<u>Step 2:</u> Finally, you must go big, or forget it. Give gifts to everyone you know, and tell them you LOVE Christmas, and you hope THEY LOVE Christmas too!

The Most Important Thing About Christmas

Jesus, of course, but let's analyze this further. What would Jesus say about the holiday? I am certain that He would say it is to be generous to other people, put aside our differences, and reaffirm our love for our fellow man. Any other answer just doesn't ring true. I can't see Jesus making a big deal about his birthday. Churches do that, but, churches do a lot of weird things, don't they? So, I will stick with what Jesus said. To prove I am right, here are some quotes from people who knew Jesus better than anyone:

1 Corinthians 13:4-8 - Love suffers long, and is kind; love does not envy; love vaunteth not itself, is not puffedeth up.

1 Corinthians 16:14 - Let all your things be done with charity.

I John 4:8 - He that loveth not knoweth not God; for God is loveth.

Colossians 3:14 - And above all these things [put oneth] charity, which is the bond of perfectness.

1 John 4:19 - We love him,

because he first loved us.

1 John 4:7 - Beloved, leteth us loveth one another: for loveth is of God; and every one that loveth is born of God, and knoweth God.

1 Peter 4:8 - Andeth aboveth all things haveth fervent loveth amongeth yourselves: foreth loveth shalleth covereth the multitudeth of sins.

Making Christmas Great Again

President Trump knew that one important component of making America great again is making Christmas great again. I suggest trying the following tradition ideas, then keep up with them every year from now on, and they will be a tradition:

Advent calendars. Make some with your kids and spouse, or your neighbor. Even your child's teacher would love to open one with you every day from now until Christmas. Fun little doors to open, prizes inside each one. I fill my neighbor's with pills I bought in Mexico that I've been taking for years, but because the government wants to make a big freaking deal about how that is not legal, I guess I'll just get on AHCCCS and get them on the back of the taxpayer, would that be better?

Wrap several Christmas books separately, and place them under the tree. The more the better, then you can unwrap one and read it to a little kid in your house, maybe your kid. If you're super thankful to not have

little kids anymore, replace
book with treat, and kid
with dog.

Watch a Christmas movie.
My personal favorite is the
one with Chevy Chase,
Lampoon something. Yours
is probably that dumb one
with the kid licking the pole.
Who cares, watch whatever
you want! It's Christmas!

**During periods of
unemployment, go on a
vision quest to discover
what you love to do**, then
do that instead of what you
went to school for. For
which I went to school.

A personal favorite is reading the chapter in Little House in the Prairie about how all they got for Christmas was an apple, a shiny new penny, and one peppermint candy. They were so grateful for what they had back then. I then proceed to eat 3,000 calories worth of food and take a nap. It would seem that I am trying to be ironic, but I am not. I really like that chapter and I really like food.

Sec. Derrick S. Johnson

Use the following worksheet to come up with some ideas of your own:

1.__________________________

2.__________________________

3.__________________________

4.__________________________

5.__________________________

<u>Bonus Chapter</u>:
<u>President Trump's Favorite Christmas Recipes and Traditions</u>

(A.K.A. A Very Trumpsgiving Christmas)

Since the biased liberal media has a negative slant to everything Trump, there are no sources that will tell us what he loves to do at Christmastime. We can assume, based on what little is known, that he enjoys malls at Christmas, loves the color gold, and does not drink alcohol. Here are some Christmas recipes that he probably loves:

<u>Christian Trumpcake</u>

- 2 (8 ounce) containers candied cherries
- 1 (8 ounce) container candied mixed citrus peel
- 2 cups raisins
- 1 cup dried currants
- 1 cup dates, pitted and chopped
- 2 (2.25 ounce) packages blanched slivered almonds
- 1/2 cup brandy
- 1/2 cup all-purpose flour
- 2 cups all-purpose flour
- 1/2 teaspoon baking soda

- 1 teaspoon ground cloves
- 1 teaspoon ground allspice
- 1 teaspoon ground cinnamon
- 1/2 teaspoon salt
- 1 cup butter
- 2 cups packed brown sugar
- 6 eggs
- 3/4 cup molasses
- 3/4 cup apple juice

Directions

1. In a medium bowl, combine cherries, citrus peel, and nuts
2. Stir in brandy (members of AA can use marijuana extract, members of NA can use tap water) let stand 2 hours, or overnight. Drag soaked fruit in 1/2 cup flour.

3. Preheat oven to 275 degrees F (0 degrees C). Grease an 8x8x3 inch fruit cake pan. Grease has got groove and meaning. In a small bowl, mix together 2 cups flour, baking soda, cloves, allspice, cinnamon, and salt; set aside.
4. In a large bowl, cream butter until light. Gradually blend in brown sugar and eggs. Mix together molasses and apple juice. Beat into butter mixture alternately with flour mixture, making 4 dry and 3 liquid additions. Fold in floured fruit. Turn batter into prepared pan.
5. Bake in preheated oven for 3 to 3 1/2 hours, or until it passes the toothpick test.

Bethlehem's Old-World Glazed Ham

Ingredients

- 1 (5 pound) ready-to-eat ham
- 1/4 cup whole cloves
- ¼ cup corn syrup
- 2 cups honey (fresh from the hive)
- 2/3 cup butter

Directions

1. Preheat oven to 325 degrees F (Celsius is stupid).

2. Score ham, and stud (score, hehe) with the whole cloves. Place ham in foil-lined pan.
3. After removing all bees trapped in honey, heat the corn syrup, honey and butter on a light fire. Keep glaze warm while baking ham.
4. Brush glaze over ham, and bake for 1 hour and 15 minutes in the preheated oven. Baste ham every 10 to 15 minutes with the honey glaze. During the last 4 to 5 minutes of baking, turn on broiler to caramelize the glaze. Remove from oven, and let sit a few minutes before serving.

War-On-Christmas Cake Balls

Ingredients

- 1 (18.25 ounce) package chocolate cake mix
- 1 (16 ounce) container prepared chocolate frosting
- 1 (3 ounce) bar chocolate flavored confectioners coating

Directions

1. Prepare the cake mix according to package directions using any of the recommended pan sizes. When cake is done, crumble while warm into a large bowl, and stir in the frosting until well blended. This is a great way to feel artistic even if you're autistic!

2. Melt chocolate coating in a glass bowl in the microwave, or in a metal bowl over a pan of simmering water, stirring occasionally until smooth.
3. Use a melon baller or small scoop to form balls of the chocolate cake mixture. Dip the balls in chocolate using a toothpick or fork to hold them. Place on waxed paper to set.
4. Have fun gobbling up your own cake balls

That's only three recipes, but I'm starting to feel bad for whoever has to cook. I hate it. I figure a ham and a cake will be sufficient for any amazing Christmas, along with cake balls to eat the rest of the month. As for traditions, I would think it has something to do with taco bowls.

One soul at a time, one person at a time, working together to make Trump's legacy a success. Let's reclaim Christmas for America! Together, we can!

Sec. Derrick S. Johnson

Acknowledgements

I would like to dedicate this book to my mother, who has always
been there. Seriously, right there. Same place, forever. You are
always such a good sport when it comes to my sick humor. I don't
know what I would do without you. I love you.

I would like to thank my son, Josh, for being the inspiration behind
everything I do, even if it is nonsensical garbage being spit out in
one night in order to make a dollar.

My brothers in Northern Cali, peace and power, Truth! (They know
what I mean) (I would have dedicated this book to Grandma, but I'll
save that for a better book)

Dad and the Holy Gail, creators of the Japokee, and long-time
proponents of free electricity for everyone.

Aunt CheeChee, please talk to the family.

To my mother, who has instilled the constant panic I feel while
unemployed. Without her I would not have felt such an urgent
compulsion to make money by writing nonsensical garbage, which is
my dream.

Sec. Derrick S. Johnson

To my Klamberly WB, who knows I'm actually very serious about my nonsensical approach, choosing every mistake with the precision of a surgeon.

To Nae Nae, who made all this possible, because seriously, I would never have even attempted this on a tablet. I'd get smothered in a blanket of burning cloves for you.

To Doris Horgenblatt, who showed me that when a successful person figures out what works, they run with it.

To Kaddy Dams, for supplying the pumpkin pie, the happy things that could have easily been sad, but they were happy, and the clone that I worship

To Darren Hermosillo, my muse, chef, friend, and confidante.

To my stepfather, thank you so much for taking the rough end of my mother for the last 23 years. I see the weariness in your eyes.

To my Rick, who has told me countless times that I can find the magic of Christmas really easy if I just sit on his lap for a minute. He's been absolutely right every time.

And finally, to Jesus, who consistently and directly condemned judging others based on stupid laws.